ABOUT THE AUTHOR

Dionne Haynes spent most of her childhood in Plymouth, England. She graduated from medical school in London and enjoyed a career as a doctor for over twenty years. After returning to Plymouth, she traded medicine for a career writing historical fiction. Dionne enjoys writing stories about ordinary people in extraordinary circumstances.

NOVELS BY DIONNE HAYNES
Running With The Wind
The Winter Years
The Second Mrs Thistlewood
Mawde of Roseland

For more books and updates:
www.dionnehaynes.com

WINDS OF CHANGE

DIONNE HAYNES

Allium

Published by Allium Books 2019
22 Victoria Road, St Austell, Cornwall, PL25 4QD

Copyright © Dionne Haynes 2019

First published by Allium Books in 2019

A CIP catalogue record for this book is available from the British Library

Paperback ISBN:978-1-9162109-0-5
eBook ISBN: 978-1-9162109-7-4
Audiobook ISBN: 978-1-9162109-8-1

For my family

CHAPTER 1

1613

Desire was afraid of water. Not the plump drops that spilled from the sky and quenched the thirst of fruit trees and golden wheat. It was deep water that scared her. The large slithering mass of the River Yare as it crept towards the sea, devouring fallen branches and stirring up silty clouds from the river bed. Occasionally it spat out a body, bloated and bedraggled. Usually an animal, but not always. Desire's parents said she was foolish. The river was essential to everyday life, providing food to fill their bellies and a transport route for trade. But Desire found the river moody. Sometimes it was placid, the surface flat like glass, with coloured stones and darting fish deep beneath the water. Other times it was menacing and grey, threatening to engulf anything brave enough to probe the choppy surface.

She turned away from the crowded riverbank and skipped along a muddy rutted lane, a freshly baked loaf of bread hugged to her chest and a bolt of brown woollen cloth tucked under one arm, both given as part payment for her mother's midwifery services to a merchant's wife. When Desire arrived at her home, she lingered outside. Raised voices drifted through the window. She stared at her shoes and sighed. Their tempers would worsen when they saw the new scuffs on the mud-spattered leather.

She took a deep breath, then thrust open the front door. 'Mother, look what Master Royce sent this time.' Desire bustled towards the kitchen table and arranged the goods on the waxed oak. 'He said he'll have good quality linen soon, if you're willing to wait a few more days.'

Her mother looked at her through bloodshot eyes, her face streaked with tears. 'Desire, you must pack up your possessions. There's a small trunk by your mattress. Fill it with as much as will fit, because everything else must stay behind.'

'Why?' Desire fought back the urge to shed tears of her own. Her shoulders tensed. 'Are you sending me away?' She feared she might share the fate of her closest friend who was sent into service at eleven years of age, having been deemed too hungry a mouth to feed with her parents expecting their sixth child.

Master Minter shook his head. 'That will never happen. Not while I live and breathe.'

'Promise?'

'Promise. Now, do as your mother says.'

'Yes, Father.' Desire peered up at him through misty eyes. 'Are we all going away?'

Master Minter nodded. 'We're moving to the city of Leyden in Holland. I've been offered an opportunity that I'd be a fool to refuse, and I believe the move will benefit all three of us. Leyden is larger and busier than Norwich, and will give you opportunities that don't exist here. Leyden already has an established English community, and a warm welcome awaits.'

Desire's bottom lip quivered. 'We're leaving England?'

Mistress Minter let out an exasperated sigh.

Her father narrowed his eyes. 'We are. Enough discussion. The arrangements are already in place. When you've finished packing, help your mother because she has much to do tonight. We leave at dawn tomorrow.'

Grey ripples fanned across the river. A thick mist obscured the opposite bank depriving Desire of a last glimpse of the city she called home. Small waves lapped at the side of a moored boat. Desire imagined the river breaking its fast with a few gentle licks of the hull, then splitting into great yawns and swallowing the little boat whole. The situation did not bode well – dark water shrouded in cloud, a tired old riverboat and a family fleeing the city like fugitives.

'Desire, hurry.' Her father beckoned her to board the boat. 'If you don't come now, we'll leave without you.'

Her feet stayed planted on the cobbles. Thoughts

tumbled through her mind. *Would they really leave without me? Can I stay behind?* Her legs trembled as she imagined the voyage to Holland – a ship tossed on high seas, ripped sails and passengers falling overboard never to be seen again.

'Desire! Do I have to lift you into this boat?'

She looked from her agitated father to her dejected mother. A life without them was unimaginable. Desire reached for her father's hand. The boat lurched as she placed one foot on the gunwale. Her shoe slipped on the damp wood, and she fell forward, crashing against her father and sending them both sprawling on the narrow deck.

'That's a bad sign if ever I saw one,' muttered the boatman, using an oar to steer towards the fast-flowing channel at the centre of the river. 'God help the girl and anyone who has the misfortune to sail with her. I hope for your sakes she hasn't just kicked up a storm and cursed your voyage. One thing's for sure, I wouldn't want to travel far with her.'

A rough sea crossing followed by a long carriage journey robbed Desire of her energy and appetite. By the time they arrived at Leyden, she was in no mood for the kind faces of strangers eager to greet them. Instead, she shrank into a corner of the room that comprised their new family home and watched her parents share food and ale with their neighbours.

During the months that followed, Desire struggled to settle and became miserable and withdrawn. The lively city was overwhelming, and the canals taunted her with their long dark ribbons of water. Day after day, she dreamed of returning to Norwich.

CHAPTER 2

1614

'DESIRE, WAKE UP.'

Bleary-eyed, Desire made out the shape of her mother amid the gloom.

'Put your clothes on. You're coming with me.'

'Where are we going?' Desire dragged her dress over her crumpled smock and stuffed her long wavy tendrils of hair beneath a linen cap.

'You've been moping around for months now, and it can't continue. It's time you worked with me as my assistant.'

Desire's mood lifted. Her mother was a reputable midwife for the church congregation, and demand for her services was spreading through the city. It would be a joy to work alongside her.

They hurried along deserted streets, passing canals painted silver by the moonlight.

Desire kept her mother nearest the water.

'Why are you still afraid?' asked her mother.

'Because we often hear about merchant ships lost at sea, or drunken young men falling into canals and drowning. Water claims so many innocent lives; therefore, I'm wary of it.'

'There are probably more dangers on land. Tonight you'll witness one of the greatest dangers that women must face repeatedly.'

Desire shrugged. 'Childbirth's a different kind of danger. Water can't be trusted. Remember our voyage from England and how ill I became? We never know how water will behave or what evil it intends. One day I'll sail back to England, and after that I'll never travel by boat again.'

Her mother smiled. 'You're too young to make such a bold statement. Ah, here we are.'

The door suddenly flew open, and a dishevelled gentleman stood before them wringing his hands.

'Mistress Minter, at last you're here. Come in, come in. Mary is in a terrible state. She's upstairs.'

The long loud moan of a woman in labour reverberated around them. The gentleman paled.

'No cause for panic, Master Allerton.' Mistress Minter gave a small smile. 'I know it's unsettling to see your wife in pain, but you mustn't worry.'

'But I don't recall such distress when our son was born.'

'No doubt the memory was replaced by the joy of seeing him for the first time. Now leave us be. My daughter will assist me and call you if we need anything.'

Desire stared at the woman on the truckle bed, her

belly swollen and taut. Submitting to another wave of pain, Mistress Allerton clenched her fingers turning her knuckles white. A prolonged groan came from deep within her chest. It reminded Desire of the cows in Norfolk, mooing to their calves.

She stifled a giggle. 'Why does she sound like a cow, Mother?'

Mistress Minter beckoned Desire to move nearer. 'Lay your hand where mine is. Next time Mistress Allerton makes that noise, you'll understand why.' The midwife patted Mistress Allerton on the arm. 'Now then, Mary, I'll examine you down below and see what progress you're making.'

Desire closed her eyes and concentrated. Skin slid against her fingertips, and Mistress Allerton let out another long groan. Muscle shifted and tightened beneath the skin. Desire snatched her hand away and stepped back from the bed. She glared at her mother.

Mistress Minter chuckled. 'So you felt it then. Put your hand back where it was, and you'll feel her womb relax while it prepares for another contraction. They're coming close together now so the babe will be here soon.'

Desire observed Mistress Allerton's face for a sign that another contraction might be building. Mistress Allerton's eyelids were closed. Her brow glistened in the candlelight, and tiny beads of sweat lined her upper lip.

She opened her eyes and reached for Desire's hand. 'You're a good girl to help your mother like this.' She tightened her grip, crushing Desire's fingers between her own, clamping them together until the contraction eased.

Desire broke free from her grasp and soaked a cloth in cool water before gently dabbing at Mistress Allerton's brow.

After several minutes of pushing and panting, a baby slithered onto the midwife's lap. Mistress Minter cut the umbilical cord. After wiping the baby clean, she wrapped her in a small sheet and passed her to her mother.

Desire beamed at the newborn and then at Mistress Allerton. 'A lovely baby girl. A beautiful reward after you were so brave.'

'I wasn't brave,' said Mistress Allerton, closing her eyes. 'It was my God-given duty to deliver my child into the world. I was fortunate to have a skilled midwife like your mother by my side.'

Desire smiled and helped Mistress Minter tidy away bloodied sheets and replace them with clean ones.

'Mother, I want to become a midwife. Will you teach me?'

Mistress Minter beamed at her daughter. 'It will be a pleasure. Now, fetch Master Allerton. He'll be eager to know that all is well.'

While Master and Mistress Allerton admired their new daughter, Desire helped her mother out of her apron, then gathered together her scissors, twine and squares of cloth. She packed them neatly in a leather drawstring bag ready for when they would be needed again.

Before leaving the room, Desire hesitated in the doorway. 'What will you name your baby?' She asked.

Master Allerton stroked the baby's cheek with his index finger. 'Her name is Remember.'

Desire smiled. 'I don't think I'll ever forget.'

She followed her mother down the stairs and outside into the sunlit street.

~

'Pack your things. We have to go.'

Desire's face dropped. 'Again, Father? Where this time?'

Master Minter grinned. 'You sound disappointed. Do you enjoy living here now?'

'In Leyden? Yes. Apart from the canals. And I enjoy working with Mother.'

'Then it's just as well we're not leaving the city. We're moving to a home of our own, and I'm confident you'll approve.'

Desire gasped and looked at her mother. 'Did you know about this?'

Mistress Minter smiled. 'Yes, but I didn't want to spoil the surprise. We must hurry. Master Tinker has loaned us a handcart but needs it back by this evening.'

Their new home was ten minutes walk away, nestled within a row of similar houses facing a narrow canal. It was spread over three floors, and Desire was thrilled to be given her own bedchamber.

'If the Lord blesses us with more children, you must share,' warned her mother.

'I know,' said Desire, smiling. For twelve years she had been an only child so a brother or sister seemed unlikely.

CHAPTER 3

1617

DESIRE SPENT many hours in her bedroom on the top floor of the house. In the evenings, she read by candle-light. By day she watched the boatmen on the canal transporting food and paper, livestock and cloth. She still feared the water, but relished the vibrant, friendly atmosphere of the city, and considered it as home – at least until she could return to England.

'Desire, we've been summoned.'

'Coming, Mother.' Desire placed her book beneath her pillow before snuffing her candle and grasping a cloak from a hook secured to the bedchamber door. She hurried down the stairs, the cloak flapping out behind her, and met her mother by the front door.

'You've assisted me well for over three years now. It's time for you to deliver a baby by yourself.'

Desire gasped. 'Thank you,' she said, wrapping her arms around her mother and holding her tight. She snatched her mother's bag from a small table and stepped outdoors into a sharp blast of icy wind.

It was unusually quiet for the house of a woman in labour. Desire glanced at her mother. Mistress Minter stood with a straight back, head held high, her expression serene. Calmed by her mother's demeanour, Desire knocked on the door. When the door opened Desire felt a lurch in her chest. A handsome young man stood beaming at her, his grey eyes twinkling.

Mistress Minter nudged Desire's arm.

'Oh, forgive me,' said Desire, stumbling over her words, her cheeks burning. 'We're the midwives.'

The young man beckoned them in. Desire stepped forward, unable to draw her eyes from him. His straw-coloured curls, delightfully untidy, framed a cherubic face flushed from wind and sun. His lips lifted at the corners, hinting at contentment. She imagined how plain she must appear to him with her pale complexion and wayward auburn hair that refused to stay tucked beneath her cap. The young man met her gaze and raised his eyebrows. Desire lowered her head and untied her cape, hoping he could not see the rosiness in her cheeks.

'Please direct us to the labouring mother.' Desire cringed at the prim tone of her voice.

'Adriana's in here,' he said, showing them into a small room next to the kitchen.

'She's so still and quiet.' Desire lowered her voice to a whisper. 'Are we too late?'

Her mother smiled. 'No, my dear. You've seen

enough deliveries to know that labour is exhausting. This is her first pregnancy, so she didn't know what to expect before the contractions began. The experience has drained her. She's dozing.'

With that, Adriana opened her eyes and nodded a greeting to the midwives. Then she puckered her brow and drew her knees towards her belly, with a guttural growl.

The labour progressed without complications. Desire beamed as she presented the young mother with her baby – a perfectly formed little boy cocooned in a soft blanket. Desire's thoughts returned to the young man. She was eager to see him again.

'Adriana, shall I fetch your husband?'

Adriana's face fell, and she shook her head.

Desire frowned. 'He must be eager to meet his son.'

'Let her have a few moments to relish the gift of her baby, Desire. Adriana may not feel ready for visitors yet.'

'It's not that.' Adriana shifted position on her mattress. 'Henri's not my husband.'

Henri. Desire repeated his name over and over in her mind.

'My husband is away negotiating a trade contract. He's not due back for three weeks.' Adriana's English was heavily accented, but otherwise faultless. 'Henri is my brother,' she added with a smile. 'No doubt he's impatient to see his nephew.'

Desire stood facing Henri, hands behind her back and fingers intertwined, praying he would not notice her trembling. 'Adriana would like to introduce you to your nephew.'

Henri grinned and clapped his hands. 'A boy! That is the most wonderful news.' He looked into Desire's eyes. 'Thank you for taking good care of my sister.'

Desire smiled. He also spoke with an accent, although milder than his sister's, suggesting many months in the company of Englishmen. Desire wished she could spend more time listening to words tumble from his lips. Henri's arm brushed against Desire's as he hurried by. For several seconds, she remained still, reliving the featherlight touch of his sleeve against hers. Then she followed him into the birthing room.

'Careful,' said Adriana, handing the mewling bundle to Henri. 'I don't want your callused hands scratching his skin before he's even a day old.' She turned her head towards Desire. 'Henri works as a stonemason.'

Desire watched Henri rock the baby back and forth, speaking with words she did not recognise. Her eyes drifted to his jacket and breeches. He was dressed in his work clothes, the coarse cloth shimmering from fine dust embedded in the weave.

'What are you working on, Master Foyon?' said Mistress Minter.

'We're making repairs to the arches at the Pieterskirk.' Henri puffed out his chest. 'And they've asked me to carve a new statue.'

Adriana chuckled. 'Forgive my brother for the sin of pride. He is the youngest stonemason to be awarded such an important commission.'

Mistress Minter nodded her approval at Henri.

Desire approached Adriana. 'It's time we left. Send word if you need us for anything.'

As she walked from the room, Henri's voice brought her to a halt. 'Thank you.'

Desire turned towards him and looked him in the eyes. She gave a slight dip of her head then hurried after her mother.

CHAPTER 4

1617

DESIRE STOOD in the shade cast by a large laburnum tree and watched the church door for hints of movement. Minutes passed. No sign of him. She strained her ears, listening for the sharp clang of metal against stone. Nothing. Even the birds were silent. Dark clouds assembled, and the air cooled. Disappointed, Desire raised the hood of her cloak and hurried home.

'Off out for another of your walks?'

Desire frowned. 'Do you mind?'

'Not at all.' Mistress Minter smiled. 'Do you like it here now?'

'I do. When I'm walking, I see familiar faces that make me feel as if I belong here. One day I'll return to England, but the yearning is less intense.'

Mistress Minter gazed through the window. 'It's a perfect day for spending time outdoors. Shall I come with you?'

Desire hesitated. 'Please do. I'd be glad of your company, Mother.'

Mistress Minter raised her eyebrows. 'Do I sense reluctance?'

'No, not at all. You caught me by surprise. It's the first time you've ever suggested coming with me.'

'And now I believe I made the offer in haste. Your father asked me to run an errand for him so I should attend to that, lest I forget all about it. Go. Enjoy the sunshine while it lasts.'

Desire kissed her mother on the cheek. 'Another time then.'

The sun was high in the sky. Trees dappled the ground with leafy shadows, and passersby greeted each other with smiles. Desire sat across from the church, admiring the tall arched windows filled with coloured glass. The sounds of workmen remained absent.

'May I join you?'

Desire used her hand to shield her eyes from the sun and squinted up at her companion. Her heart fluttered when she saw who it was. 'I'd be glad of your company.'

Henri brushed dust from his breeches before settling beside her. 'Are you expecting someone?'

Desire shook her head.

'Pity. I was hoping you were waiting for me.'

Desire giggled. 'Why would I do such a thing?'

Henri shrugged. 'A young man can dream.'

'How are your sister and nephew?'

'Both are very well, thank you. My brother-in-law is home, and he's a very proud father.'

Desire sensed Henri's eyes on her. Her cheeks bloomed. Heart pounding, she tilted her face towards him. They held each other's gaze, a comfortable silence settling between them.

Several minutes passed with few words exchanged.

'I regret that I must return to work already.'

'In there?' Desire pointed at the church.

'Not today. I'm based in a workshop nearby while working on a statue of an angel. Would you like to see it when it's finished?'

'I'd love to.' A hollow feeling settled deep in her stomach. She wanted him to stay longer.

'I have the afternoon free on Sunday. Meet me here at two?'

Desire nodded.

Henri scrambled to his feet and gave a slight bow. 'Think of me. I'll be counting down the hours until then.' He dipped his head then scurried away, his cap scrunched in one hand.

As bells announced the hour, Henri linked Desire's arm through his. 'For months now, we have walked the same route every Sunday. Today, we will go a different way. I have something special to show you.'

Desire glanced over her shoulder to see if her parents were still following.

Henri chuckled. 'Our Sunday shadows. A treat for them, too.'

'Where are we going?'

'It's a surprise. Be patient. You'll find out soon enough.'

Desire tensed as they stepped on to the bridge to cross the Steenschuur.

Henri tutted. 'This fear of yours is irrational. The canals and rivers are no threat to you. You are probably safer on a canal than on a street.'

Desire's breaths came fast and shallow, her hands and knees trembled. 'My parents often say the same. But I'm petrified of drowning.'

'But why? It makes little sense.' Henri's accent was more pronounced, hinting at frustration.

Midway across the bridge Desire stopped and rested her forearms on the rail. She screwed her eyelids tight and forced herself to breathe more slowly. When she opened her eyes, she looked at the canal. Sunlight dappled on the crests of ripples, sparkling like polished diamonds. The water reflected the blue sky, soft clouds, and leafy trees overhanging the canal's edge. Rows of houses with stepped gables stood sentinel on either side, windows open to welcome the balmy April breeze. Couples crowded the pathways, enjoying the warm spring day, the canal equally busy with boats filled with pleasure-seekers. The air was rich with happiness and optimism.

'I don't know why it scares me so. But seeing these men and women laughing and chattering on their boats makes me feel so much better. I'm half-tempted to join them.' And to her surprise, she meant it.

Henri beamed. 'I knew it. When the crowds thin, we will enjoy a short boat trip together on the canal. I'll prove to you once and for all that you have nothing to fear. But for now, come with me. We are close to our destination.'

'Already? We've walked such a short distance.'

'So often it's the case that we need not travel far to admire great beauty.'

Desire slipped her hand around Henri's upper arm and allowed Henri to lead her off the bridge. They passed magnificent red brick buildings of the city's university and followed a high wall until they came to a door.

Henri reached for the handle and paused. 'Ready?'

'Ready.'

Henri turned the handle and nudged the door open. He stepped forward and beckoned for Desire to follow him. She peered past Henri and squealed with joy.

Henri gave her a shy smile. 'Welcome to the Hortus Botanicus. I knew you'd like it.'

Desire's eyes roved back and forth. There were countless flower beds laid out in neat geometric patterns, the vivid blooms basking in sunlight.

'Come. The best view is in that far corner.'

Henri took Desire's hand and drew her beneath an archway of delicate white flowers. They turned a corner and passed a screen of bushes before coming to an area of garden enclosed by a low fence.

'Tulips,' said Desire recognising the intensely coloured red and yellow petals bobbing in the breeze.

'Tulips,' echoed Henri, grinning. 'But not just any tulips. Follow me. We have permission to step inside and look more closely.'

A gardener beckoned Henri to join him a few rows from the gate. Henri gestured that Desire should lead. She picked her way between the flowerbeds, taking care not to brush against any flowers with her skirt. When she reached the gardener, she cried out in surprise.

'Henri! These tulips have stripes! It's as if they're on fire.'

Desire fell to her knees and cradled a tulip flower in her hands. Deep red gave way to harsh bright yellow within the same petal, the texture waxy, and gleaming in the sunlight.

Henri raised Desire to her feet and turned her to face him. 'Some day I'll build homes for the people of Leyden. My trademark will be to plant these tulips in the garden or a window-box of every house I build. They will be my signature. I'm not yet in circumstances that allow me to begin this venture, but when I do, Desire, I want you in my life.'

Desire's cheeks flushed. 'Are you asking me to marry you?'

Henri grasped both her hands in his. 'I am. Your father has given his permission, although he insists we wait until my finances are in order and you are past your nineteenth birthday. He is right to stipulate these things, but I need to know if you will become my wife one day?'

'Yes, Henri. I will.'

Henri hugged Desire to him. Desire inhaled the musky scent of his skin mingled with the dust ingrained in his clothes. His warm, protective arms enveloped her. She caught her father's eye and smiled. William Minter nodded and smiled back.

Henri loosened his embrace and rested his large hands on Desire's shoulders. 'Shall we go for a ride on the canal to celebrate our betrothal and our trust in one another?'

Desire clasped his hands in hers. 'Henri, I will gladly ride on the canal with you by my side, and I will enjoy every moment.'

A cold breeze whipped around Desire's ankles, swirling dust and leaf debris across her shoes.

Henri sighed. 'My late grandmother used to say that when the wind blows dust in circles, a change is in the air. I teased her for such foolishness. Now it seems she was right.'

Desire grasped Henri's hand and allowed him to lead her away from the graveyard. Eyes misted with sorrow, she watched the hunched figure of her widowed mother shuffle towards them and stumble on small stones. Henri slipped his hand from Desire's and hurried to Mistress Minter's side. He grasped her by the elbow, preventing her from crumpling to the path. Desire took her mother's other arm, then the three of them led a solemn procession home.

CHAPTER 5

1618

'MASTER SIMMONS ASKED me to become his wife. I said yes.' Mistress Minter sat with her hands clasped together on the kitchen table.

Desire glared at her mother. 'What? Father mere months in his grave and already cast from your mind. Are you not ashamed?'

'No, Desire, not at all.' A tear trickled from Mistress Minter's left eye. 'Your father was a wonderful husband, and I will always cherish him, but as a widow I must be practical. It's difficult for a woman on her own. Master Simmons is a kind man and was a dear friend of William's. The proposal of marriage offers security, and only a fool would reject him.'

'But with us both working as midwives, we can afford to live well. Mother, you have no need of another husband.'

Mistress Minter stared into the distance. Desire felt

icy fingers of dread tighten around her chest. 'There's something else, isn't there?'

Mistress Minter nodded. 'There are more midwives in the community now, so we cannot guarantee a sufficient income.' She reached for Desire's hand. 'Sometimes mothers have to make difficult choices and do things they once considered unthinkable. I haven't been able to keep up payments on the loan your father took out to buy this house, so I had to make such a choice. I must sell our home. Master Simmons has no desire to delay our marriage and so, by the grace of God, I will become Mistress Simmons twelve weeks from now and take up residence in his house.'

Desire opened and closed her mouth, temporarily lost for words.

'Be joyful for me, Desire. It was a difficult decision, but I made a choice that I believe will benefit both of us.'

'It's kind of Master Simmons to take us in.' Desire heard her mother's sharp intake of breath. 'Oh, Mother, tell me I'm to go with you?'

Mistress Minter clenched her lips together in a thin line and shook her head. 'I'm so sorry. I had no other options.'

Desire felt a tightness in her chest. 'So what will become of me? Will you cast me on to the streets?'

'Dearest daughter, I could never do that to you. I've secured a position for you with the printer, Thomas Brewer. He promised to treat you well.'

Desire swept her arm across the table sending a plate

and mug clattering to the stone floor. 'I'm to go into service?'

'Please, don't shout,' sobbed Mistress Minter. 'Don't you think I've suffered enough? I'm doing my best to provide for you. You're sixteen years old, Desire. Time moves fast. Before long, Henri will give you a home of your own. Master Brewer knows of your plans and generously agreed to a four year arrangement instead of something longer term.'

'Four years! That's too long.' Desire's pulse throbbed in her ears. 'How could you?' She thrust her chair back and fled the kitchen, sobbing.

'Please, Henri. Do something. If you love me, you'll find a way of marrying me sooner.'

Henri chewed his bottom lip. 'I'll find a way to earn more money and bring our marriage forward.'

'Can't we marry now? We could live with your sister.'

Henri stroked Desire's damp cheeks. 'Alas, that is not our solution. Adriana already carries the burden of caring for my parents, and she is expecting her second child. Her house is not large enough for us and our children too.'

Desire's mood softened at the thought of bearing Henri's children. 'What are we to do?'

Henri smiled. 'It's summer. I can work late into the evenings and Sunday afternoons. We'll have little or no time together, but it's only temporary. With private commissions, I can save enough to set up a home perhaps as soon as two years from now.'

'Pray that Master Brewer will release me from his service by then.'

Henri grinned. 'If there's a child in your belly he will. Let us walk by the canal. After today, opportunities for such pleasures will be rare.'

Desire paced her small bedchamber at the top of Master Brewer's house. The room was sparsely furnished but comfortable and overlooked a narrow canal. Desire gazed at the water, tiny ripples skidding across the surface as a breeze gathered strength. She smiled. Henri's workshop backed onto the same canal. It was as if the waterway joined them together.

'Henri?' Desire pressed her face to the cool glass windowpane.

The familiar silhouette scurried along the road, head bowed. Something was wrong. Henri usually greeted passersby and watched Desire's window ready to wave if he glimpsed her shadow. Desire ran down the stairs and flung the door wide open.

'Henri? What's happened? Is it your mother? Your sister? Pray, God, not one of the children!'

Henri turned his sad face towards her. 'May I come in?'

Desire nodded. 'Mistress Brewer is visiting her daughter. She'll be out until late afternoon.'

Desire poured them each an ale, then sat at the table, expectant.

Henri let out a long breath. 'I don't know how to break the news to you.'

'Please, just say it as it is.'

Henri fixed his eyes on Desire's face. 'I have important news which has muddled my emotions.'

Desire raised her hands, imploring him to continue.

'I must travel to Spain.'

'Why?'

'To carve angels for the cathedral in Toledo. They've commissioned several new sculptures and have requested me for my skills. I will be paid handsomely for my work.'

'How long will you stay there?'

Henri pursed his lips. 'I cannot say. Eighteen months. Maybe two years.' He intertwined his fingers with Desire's. 'But when I return I'll have enough money to marry you, so it's not all bad news.'

'Will you travel by sea?'

Henri nodded. 'It's the fastest way to reach northern Spain. Then we'll be on horseback. Two of us are to travel together, so I'll not be alone. I'll send word when we get there, so you'll know the sea has not devoured me.'

Desire giggled. 'You make a fool of me. Thanks to you, I'm no longer afraid.'

'I know. And I'm pleased, for it's the sea that will bring me home to you.'

'When do you leave?'

'In two weeks. I have one commission piece to finish, then my evenings are yours if you can spend time with me.'

'My master and mistress are reasonable people so they'll not stop you crossing their threshold. They'll know that with you in Spain and my mother remarried I'll not want time to myself for the foreseeable future.'

Henri cupped her face in his hands. 'You'll be with me every day, Desire, in my thoughts and in my heart.'

Desire smiled. 'And you in mine.'

CHAPTER 6

1619

POUNDING ON THE DOOR. Shouts. Words in a language Desire did not understand. She glanced at Mistress Brewer and knew at once something terrible was happening.

'Who can it be?' said Desire frowning.

Mistress Brewer turned her ashen face towards Desire. 'This is the end. We're finished.'

Master Brewer scraped his chair across the floorboards and pushed himself to his feet. He smoothed down his breeches and straightened his jacket. 'I prayed this day would never come, but I knew the risks I was taking.'

Mistress Brewer went to her husband's side. They embraced, planting delicate kisses on one another's cheeks. When they parted, Master Brewer stood tall, hands clasped behind his back.

Mistress Brewer stood upright. She lifted her chin

and placed one hand over the other at her waist. 'Desire, bring in the visitors.'

Louder banging. More persistent. Raised voices fuelled with combatant excitement. Desire took a few deep breaths, then opened the door. A tall, fair-haired gentleman, dressed in fine quality clothes and a thick woollen cloak, eyed her up and down. He thrust Desire aside and strode towards the kitchen. Three brutish men followed, their cheeks flushed with anticipation. Desire hung back. They bore no weapons, but reeked of danger.

The leader of the group yelled a volley of words at Master Brewer.

'In English please, so my wife can understand.'

'As you wish. Master Brewer, in my capacity as an official of the University of Leyden, I am commanded by Sir Dudley Carleton, English ambassador to the Netherlands, to take you into custody. You will be charged and punished in accordance with English law. If found guilty, you will be incarcerated in the university prison.'

'My husband has committed no crime.' Mistress Brewer's voice was calm. 'Holland welcomes freedom of thinking in all matters of religion. You, of all people, should know that. How dare you invade our home with such hostility, having previously welcomed those of us persecuted in our own country.'

'Alas, Mistress Brewer, it is not your husband's ideas or beliefs that are at fault, but the fact he saw fit to print them and smuggle illegal pamphlets into England.'

Master Brewer puffed out his cheeks. 'It's wrong to dictate how a man should think.'

The official cocked his head to one side. 'It's wrong to break the law.' With a flick of his hand, two of his companions grasped Master Brewer by the arms.

Desire flattened herself against the wall as they stomped past, the man nearest her trampling across her foot. She struggled to catch her breath as they shoved her master through the door and out into the street.

'Well, that's it then.' Mistress Brewer's shoulders slumped. 'I told him to stop. Begged him. But he wouldn't listen.' Desire watched the skin flicker over Mistress Brewer's tensed jaw. 'They'll have seized the printing presses by now. Without them we have no business. I can't stay in this house, nor can I keep you with me. Consider yourself released from service to me and my husband. You have one week to make alternative arrangements. I suggest you ask your mother to take you in.'

Desire lost the strength in her legs and dropped to her knees, landing hard on the unforgiving floorboards. Mistress Brewer looked away, her face drained of colour and personality drained of warmth.

'I wondered when you'd appear on my doorstep.'

Desire frowned. 'I thought you'd be glad to see me.'

Her mother sniffed. 'When I received the news about the Brewers, I expected you soon after. That was three days ago, so when you didn't show I presumed you had no wish to spend time with your mother. You're here now, so come inside.'

Mistress Simmons showed her to a chair by the hearth. Wood lay stacked in the grate ready for when the chill settled later in the evening.

'Mother, I wanted to come and see you but couldn't bear the thought of having to leave you again afterwards.'

Mistress Simmons sniffed. 'The printer agreed to you having two free Sunday afternoons per month. Such regular visits would have softened the pain of each parting. Was it too much to ask for you to visit your mother during your leisure time?'

'Was it too much to ask for my mother to visit me after casting me adrift with little warning?'

Mistress Simmons bristled. 'Your master has encouraged poor manners. Never have I heard you speak with such disrespect.'

Desire gazed towards the window. Heavy rain clouds darkened the sky. A tree rustled as an autumn wind stirred. Withered leaves parted from branches and danced and looped in the air before being tossed to the other side of the road.

'Please God, not another wind of change,' mumbled Desire.

'What was that?'

'Henri's grandmother used to say that when the wind causes dust or leaves to swirl in circles, it predicts a change is coming.'

'I presume he meant more than a change in the weather.' Mistress Simmons softened her tone. 'There's a storm brewing by the looks of things.'

'Mother, I'm sorry I didn't visit. But after Father's passing, and your remarrying so soon afterwards... it was too much for me.'

'I had no choice. One day you'll understand.' Mistress Simmons lowered her head. 'Not a day passes without me mourning for your father. He was the best of all men. My new husband is a good man, but he's not William.'

'Mother, I have a problem. Because of the unfortunate events for the Brewers, Mistress Brewer is moving out of the house at the end of the week, and I must leave too. May I stay here for a while? I'll do whatever you ask of me – chores around the house, deliver babies, work for Master Simmons – anything to be with you. We've already spent so much time apart, and we never did go for that walk.'

'Desire, it breaks my heart to deny you, but it's not possible.'

A sneeze alerted them to the presence of Master Simmons. He sidled through the doorway and glared at Desire.

'Your mother and I have an appointment, so I regret that you must leave.'

Desire glimpsed a flicker of confusion cross her mother's brow.

'Yes, the appointment. How careless of me to forget.

Thank you for visiting, Daughter, and sharing your news. Please come again soon.'

'But, Mother, what about my predicament?'

Master Simmons placed a firm hand on his wife's shoulder. 'Wife, you cannot have forgotten to tell her about the new arrangement?'

'What do you mean?' Desire wrinkled her brow. 'What arrangement?'

'Your mother sold you into service with Thomas Brewer, but because he was arrested before paying in full, the foolish printer still owes her money. Fortunately my wife is a cunning businesswoman and she has found someone else willing to take on the debt.'

'Is this true?' Bile burned at the back of Desire's throat. Her stomach clenched, and the room appeared to tilt. 'Mother, what have you done?'

'Dearest Desire, it's for your own good. John Carver has agreed to take you. He's a pleasant man, a prominent member of the community and respected by everyone. And I know your father would approve of what I've done.'

'I doubt that. My father promised he would never send me into service.'

Mistress Simmons rolled her eyes. 'And he kept his word. Your father didn't send you into service, I did. William would have done the same in my situation. The Carvers expect you on Sunday afternoon. Perfect timing with you having to leave Mistress Brewer on the very same day.'

Desire staggered to her feet. The room swayed and

her vision blurred. She slowed her breathing and closed her eyes waiting for the discomfort to pass. Once recovered she glared at her mother. 'I don't recognise this woman you've become. Heartless and greedy.' She turned to face Master Simmons. 'You've changed her.'

With a sad smile, she said farewell to her mother and staggered from the room. As she stepped outside, the wind whipped at her cloak and cold raindrops tumbled from the sky. Her dress and shift soon soaked through, clinging to her skin and chilling her to the bone.

CHAPTER 7

1620

Dearest Mother

Henri is dead. Dead!

A letter arrived from Toledo informing me of his terrible demise. He was installing an angel into an alcove when the scaffold gave way, and he fell thirty feet, smashing his head on the corner of a pew. I cannot believe I'll never see him again. The news has ripped my heart in two, and it's impossible to envisage a day when it will be whole again. I've lost two people dear to me – Father first, and now Henri. I pray that I have not yet lost you.

Dear Mother, please send word that I may come to you. Master Carver is as kind a master as you promised and will permit a day or two of absence to console myself in your presence.

Please, I need your love more now than ever before.

Your daughter,

Desire

~

'When do we leave?'

The conversation was muffled. Desire pressed her ear against the door.

'Early summer. I've bought shares in the joint-stock company. After seven years, the company will be liquidated and we'll receive a proportion of the profits. Life will be challenging when we first settle in America, but we'll grow accustomed to our new surroundings, and eventually reap the rewards of our labour and investment.'

'And everyone else is content with this arrangement?'

'Dearest, this move has been planned to the finest details. You've not expressed doubt before. Are you having second thoughts now?'

'No, John. As you say, it's been carefully thought out. It's taken an age to reach this point so a small part of me thought it would never happen. But it is happening, and we truly are to live in America.'

Desire blanched and pressed her hands to her mouth to prevent any noise escaping. She was fond of the Carvers and would be sorry to see them leave. She retreated to the kitchen to begin preparations for dinner.

'Desire? Come here please.'

Desire placed her knife on the table and wiped her hands on her apron.

She hurried to the parlour and lingered in the doorway. 'Yes, Mistress Carver?'

'Come in. Sit down. We have an important announcement which will come as a surprise.' She waited for Desire to get comfortable before continuing. 'A few weeks from now we're sailing to Virginia with other members of the congregation. We're going to America!'

Desire remained composed, her mind wandering to who might become her next employer. A dressmaker, perhaps. Or a prosperous merchant in need of a house-keeper. One day she would establish herself as a midwife.

She smiled at Mistress Carver. 'That is good news. It's an exciting opportunity, and I'm sure you'll make the best of it.'

Mistress Carver clapped her hands. 'I can hardly believe it. I confess to being a little on edge, but it's a dream come true. So long in the planning and finally coming to fruition. And it pleases me to tell you that although you haven't been with us long, we value your service and we're taking you too.'

Desire could not breathe. Words caught in her throat, threatening to choke her.

Master Carver chuckled. 'Wife, you have rendered her speechless.'

'Desire, you're an absolute treasure. Hardworking, loyal, and the tidiest person I know.' Mistress Carver chuckled. 'If not for you, my husband's papers would be in permanent disarray.'

'Can't argue with that.' Master Carver smiled.

'Desire, you deserve to share this adventure. You've already faced adversity with courage, and you're a fine young woman. You will fare well in America. The other servants are coming too, so you'll not be alone. Use an hour or two to make sense of the news before you return to work, after all, it's a lot to take in.'

Desire wandered the streets of Leyden, eyes fixed on the dusty ground, oblivious to everyone around her. The May sunlight warmed the back of her neck, and sweat dampened her dress. Her longing for England was intense. She lifted her head and was surprised to see her mother's home in front of her. Believing fate led her there, she decided it was time to make amends.

Desire approached the door and raised her hand to knock. She hesitated. Something was wrong. Chiding herself for being foolish, she rapped hard, turning her knuckles red. A hacking cough sounded inside the house. Desire feared for her mother's well-being. The sound of a heavy bolt sliding. Then another. Something untoward must have occurred for her step-father to add such a security measure. She prayed that all was well. At last the door opened a fraction. The interior was dark, the smell old and damp.

'Mother?' Desire tried to push the door open, but felt resistance from the other side.

'Who's there?'

'Mother, it's me, Desire. Are you unwell? Your voice sounds—'

'I have no daughter. You're at the wrong house.'

Desire frowned. It was definitely the same house she had visited before. 'Mother, please, let me in.'

'I told you, you've got the wrong house.'

The door creaked open. A woman stepped into the light, her face crinkled with age, her joints gnarled. She shuffled forward, unsteady on her feet.

'Is this the house belonging to Master Simmons?'

The old woman cackled and coughed. 'Snooty Simmons left months ago. This is my son's home now.' She started to close the door.

'Wait! Where will I find my mother and her husband?'

The woman peered at Desire and sneered. 'Did rather well for themselves and moved to a bigger place. Cross the bridge behind you and take the second left. You can't miss the Simmons' house. Grandest in the street.'

The door slammed, leaving Desire startled and confused. After gathering her senses, she set off towards the bridge. If her mother was enjoying an affluent life, Desire might not have to sail to America.

Master Simmons' house was large and imposing, its four storeys built of red brick and casting an elegant reflection on a canal. Desire rushed towards it and grasped an ornamental knocker affixed to the door. Her heart lurched. The knocker was in the shape of an angel. Trying in vain to cast Henri from her mind, she knocked three times.

At first Desire did not recognise her mother.

Mistress Simmons greeted her with a radiant smile and open arms, eager to embrace her daughter. But the greatest surprise was her large distended belly.

'You look well, Mother.'

Mistress Simmons placed a hand over her unborn child. 'I am well. The baby is due in a matter of weeks. Pray God, it's a boy this time.'

Desire's face fell. 'Would another daughter be such a disappointment for you?'

Her mother's face dropped. 'Of course not. Desire, I'm sorry for how things turned out for you, but my husband was not the affable gentleman he first portrayed and refused to let me help you. But he's mellowed now that I carry his child. Come in and sit with me. Let us enjoy one another's company and swap news.'

They sat in the kitchen on hard chairs softened by plump cushions.

Desire fidgeted with the folds of her skirt. 'Why didn't you reply to my letter?'

Mistress Simmons puckered her brow. 'What letter? The old crone passed no letters to me. What did it say?'

Desire forced a smile. 'It doesn't matter now.'

She listened to the story of her mother's struggles in the early days of her marriage before her husband's unexpected change of fortune.

'So you are comfortably settled and wanting for nothing?'

Mistress Simmons nodded and leaned forward in

her chair. 'Our circumstances are far better than I could ever have hoped for. Now tell me your news.'

Desire relayed the Carvers plans to move to Virginia.

'There have been rumours for a long time. So, it's going ahead. I wish them all well and admire their bravery, selling up and moving to the New World. And it's a marvellous opportunity for you, Desire.'

Desire dropped to her knees and reached for her mother's hands. 'But I don't wish to go. I want to stay here with you. Please say you'll let me now that your husband is doing well in his business. This house is huge, there must be enough space for me. And it won't be for long. As soon as I find work I'll move into lodgings and visit during every one of my afternoons off.'

Mistress Simmons stroked Desire's tear-stained face. 'I'll have to ask—'

'The answer is no.' Master Simmons stood in the doorway, his dark-clad figure absorbing the daylight and casting a chill in the air.

'Husband, surely we can accommodate her for a short while? Desire can help care for the baby.'

'I'm good with numbers too, so if it pleases you, Master Simmons, I can help with book-keeping.'

'I don't want you prying into my affairs. This is my home and I say you cannot stay.'

Desire felt her mother's grasp tighten.

Master Simmons stepped further into the room. 'We are prosperous now, but fortunes change. I've invested a large sum in a risky venture, so cannot take you under my wing in case the gamble fails. If the Carvers are keen to take you to America, you must go.'

'But America's so far away. I may never return.'

Master Simmons shrugged. 'You may have twenty minutes to say your goodbyes. We have important guests visiting later, and your mother must finish her preparations.'

Mother and daughter clung to each other, embracing fiercely.

'Time's up.'

'Wait! There's something I wish to give Desire as a parting gift. Allow me time to find it.'

Master Simmons gave a curt nod and stood glaring at Desire until his wife returned, her progress slow and lumbering on the stairs.

'Take this.' Mistress Simmons held out a small mirror, edged with filigree. 'We share similar facial features. Every time you look in the mirror, you'll see my image looking back at you, watching over you. And take this too.' She presented a journal bound with smooth leather. 'You can write your thoughts in it, or news about your home in America. Or you may find another practical use for it.'

'Thank you, Mother.' Desire fought to keep her composure. 'I pray we'll be blessed with the good fortune to see one another again one day.'

Mistress Simmons clamped her lips together and nodded. 'I do love you, Desire, with all my heart. Please don't ever forget that.'

Her mother's words washed over her like a soothing balm.

'I love you too, Mother.' Desire's voice was little more than a whisper.

Her chest ached with sorrow. She embraced her mother one last time, then stepped outside into an uncertain future.

CHAPTER 8

1620

IT DID NOT TAKE LONG to pack the Carvers' possessions. Furniture was sold to pay for the voyage, and trinkets distributed among friends remaining in Leyden.

Desire fastened a pair of hefty buckles on the largest trunk, satisfied nothing was missing from Master Carver's list. In America, they would rely on the arrival of more ships to replenish cloth, tools and utensils. She stared at her own small trunk and wondered how her life amounted to so little. Two kirtles, a lace collar, three shifts, one pair of shoes, one apron, one shawl, a linen cap, hairbrush, mirror, journal and the clothes she was wearing. Her thoughts drifted to Henri, and she buried her face in her hands.

A choking sound pulled Desire's attention back to the room. She dabbed at her damp cheeks with her sleeve and rose to her feet. Mistress Carver sat hunched forward on a chair, rocking back and forth. Desire hurried to her side. Mistress Carver grasped Desire's hands, her sharp fingernails pricking against Desire's palms.

'Shall I fetch the master?'

Mistress Carver clamped her lips together in a thin line and shook her head more vigorously. 'My husband has worked tirelessly on this. So much time, energy and money. He has all our best interests at heart and I must not fail him.'

Desire drew one hand free from Mistress Carver's grip and stroked her mistress's arm. 'Please don't fret. Is there something I can do to help?'

Mistress Carver hung her head. 'No. My husband is right to lead us to Virginia, but it feels so final. I've had a happy life here in Leyden. Now I must leave dear friends. And how I will miss my sisters!'

Desire watched her mistress's shoulders twitch in time with her sobs. 'I too know the pain of loss,' she whispered.

Mistress Carver dried her eyes and sat straight-backed on the chair. 'I'm sorry, Desire. How selfish of me. No doubt you suffer a similar pain. Forgive me my foolishness. From now on, we will draw on each other's strength. Now, where's the Howland boy? And Roger, too. It's time they loaded the trunks onto the cart. And Dorothy. What can she be doing?'

'Dorothy's helping Master distribute the books he cannot take with him. I'll find John and Roger and make sure they've loaded the cart before Master returns.'

Mistress Carver gave a thin smile. 'I don't know what I'd do without you.'

The mood was melancholy at Pastor Robinson's house, the atmosphere charged with apprehension. Women picked at their food, while men spoke in loud voices tinged with false bravado. Children sat sullen and listless, staring into space, while Pastor Robinson gave a final sermon before the congregation would fracture. Desire withdrew towards the back of the room and sank to the dusty floor. The thought of sailing to Virginia held such great horror, the risk of storms preoccupying her mind. She tried to imagine a contented life – abundant food, a warm home, the company of friends – but the overriding fear of travelling into the unknown erased all positive thoughts from her mind. Desire drew her knees to her chest and wept.

Two processions left Leyden at dawn, one by canal, the other by road. Desire thanked God for guiding the Carvers to travel by road – soon they would be trapped within the confines of a ship. Those on horseback resisted the urge to gallop ahead. Those who walked placed one aching foot in front of the other, distracting one another with chatter and sharing their dreams. Carts and carriages rumbled along the road, rocking and shaking as they negotiated ruts and large stones.

Desire kept her eyes trained on the horizon, waiting

for a glimpse of the port. At last the tops of masts appeared, and noise filled the air. The shouts of fishermen, shipbuilders, merchants and sailors, all struggling to be heard over one another. Desire suppressed a giggle. It was as if the town was drawing her forward, pulling her towards a new life, far from sad memories and echoes of the dead. She caught a glance from Dorothy and smiled. Dorothy's taut expression softened, and she returned the smile. They linked arms and quickened their steps.

Desire scanned the ships docked in the harbour. 'I hope it's that one,' she said, nudging Dorothy and pointing to a large merchant ship.

John Howland snorted. 'You're in for a big disappointment.' He smirked and pointed to a ship docked further away. 'That's ours.'

Desire gasped. 'Are you sure? It looks so… tiny. And old.'

John shrugged. 'Ships aren't cheap you know. The *Speedwell* was probably all they could afford. Don't forget we'll meet up with another one in Southampton – the *Mayflower*, or something like that.'

Desire struggled to swallow as she imagined the small ship tossed about on large waves. 'Do you think we'll make it across the ocean?'

'What choice do we have? If Master Carver says we sail on that, as servants we're in no position to argue.' He smirked at Desire. 'Don't tell me you're scared?'

Desire sniffed haughtily. 'Why should I be afraid?'

'Desire? Dorothy?' Mistress Carver beckoned the

girls to her. 'Howland, find your master and help transfer our belongings to the ship.'

Desire watched the cart trundle away, her trunk perched on top and secured in place with a thin rope.

Mistress Carver let out a breath through pursed lips. 'Let us make our way to the ship and set up our sleeping quarters. As soon as everything's aboard, we're to gather outside the church for prayers.'

Desire stood on the main deck, feet apart, hands gripping the gunwale. She stared at her knuckles and grimaced. They were white.

Men, women and children crowded the quayside, waving and cheering, eager to give the travellers a good send-off. Desire studied their faces. Many were from Leyden, but her mother was not one of them.

Aboard ship, the noise level dropped.

Dorothy leaned in towards Desire. 'They're saying the tide has turned, and it's time to leave.'

Pastor Robinson dropped to his knees, his arms and face raised to the sky, his lips moving in fervent prayer.

Desire's breaths were fast and shallow. A roaring in her ears blocked out the pastor's voice. She clamped her eyelids shut and fought to calm her nerves.

The well-wishers fell silent, their faces streaked with tears. Jubilation gave way to desolation, and melancholy stalked the air. Desire took pity on the women around her as they succumbed to grief, struggling to leave loved ones behind. She knew their pain and vowed to do everything possible to protect herself from experiencing it again.

The master of the *Speedwell* ordered his crew to untie the ropes and raise the anchors. Sails were unfurled and filled by a breeze which carried the *Speedwell* away from its berth. Delfshaven shrank into the distance, and the ship turned into the River Maas, heading for the North Sea. A strong breeze caught Desire's cap, lifting it from her hair. She reached up and grabbed it.

'Henri,' she murmured. 'Another of your winds of change.'

The river slapped at the ship's hull. Sails flapped, and masts creaked. Desire stared at the dark river with its small jagged peaks. The waves would grow far bigger when they reached the ocean. But Desire vowed that, no matter how wild the seas became, she would place her trust in God and the memory of dear, beloved, brave Henri.

She refused to be afraid.

The story continues in the novel, Running With The Wind.

Dear Reader,

I hope you enjoyed this short story and that it left you wanting to read more about Desire.

Desire was a passenger on the famous *Mayflower* voyage of 1620. Sources tell us that she was sent into service when her mother became widowed, and she travelled to the New World as a servant to the Carver family. This fictional account is only part of her story. *Running With The Wind* tells the tale of what might have happened on that *Mayflower* voyage. Told from Jedediah Trelawney's point of view, Desire has an important role in this story too.

Have you joined the Allium Books Readers Club?

Receive a monthly newsletter, advance notification of my new releases, and a FREE novella download as a welcome gift. Visit my website at www.dion nehaynes.com.

I hope to see you there!

Dionne

P.S. I love interacting with my readers. You can connect with me on Facebook, Twitter and Instagram, or drop me a line at dionne@dionnehaynes.com

Made in the USA
Monee, IL
14 January 2024

51786573R00039